Bigger, Taller,
Heavier, Smaller

M E A S U R I N G

T E R C

Investigations in Number, Data, and Space®

Dale Seymour Publications®

Menlo Park, California

The *Investigations* curriculum was developed at TERC (formerly
Technical Education Research Centers) in collaboration with Kent State
University and the State University of New York at Buffalo. The work was
supported in part by National Science Foundation Grant No. ESI-9050210.
TERC is a nonprofit company working to improve mathematics and science
education. TERC is located at 2067 Massachusetts Avenue, Cambridge,
MA 02140.

This project was supported, in part,
by the
National Science Foundation
Opinions expressed are those of the authors
and not necessarily those of the Foundation

Managing Editor: Catherine Anderson
Series Editor: Beverly Cory
ESL Consultant: Nancy Sokol Green
Production/Manufacturing Director: Janet Yearian
Production/Manufacturing Manager: Karen Edmonds
Production/Manufacturing Coordinator: Amy Changar
Design Manager: Jeff Kelly
Design: Don Taka
Illustrations: Carl Yoshihara, Rachel Gage
Composition: Thomas A. Dvorak

This book is published by Dale Seymour Publications®, an imprint of
Addison Wesley Longman, Inc.

Dale Seymour Publications
2725 Sand Hill Road
Menlo Park, CA 94025
Customer Service: 800-872-1100

Order number DS43713
ISBN 1-57232-477-5
12 13 14 15-ML-05 04 03 02

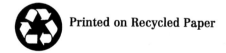

Printed on Recycled Paper

Contents

*Repeated-use sheet

Which Is Heavier?

_____ or _____

_____ or _____

_____ or _____

_____ or _____

_____ or _____

Something to Weigh

Please bring from home an object to weigh.

It should weigh less than about half a pound.

It should not be taller or wider than about 6 inches.

What did you decide to bring?

_____

_____

To the Family

Compare

Math Content
Gathering materials for exploring weight in class

Materials
Student Sheet 2
Pencil

In class, students are beginning to explore weight. We are talking about which objects "feel" heavier and lighter, and students will be comparing weights of objects with a pan balance scale. For homework, your child needs to find a small object, such as a spool of thread, a toy car, or a small stone, to bring to school to use for our weight activities. To fit in a small balance, the object should fall within the size constraints given on the student sheet. Help your child be sure that the object is small enough.

Heavier, Lighter, the Same

Choose one object to put in the balance
every time.

What is it? _____

1. Find one thing heavier.

   What is it? _____

2. Find one thing lighter.

   What is it? _____

3. Find one thing that weighs the same.

   What is it? _____

Draw a picture to show how the balance looked
for one of these three cases.

Finding Things That Balance

Get two bags (paper or plastic). Find some things in your kitchen to put in the bags. Make the two bags weigh about the same.

Hold the bags, one in each hand, the way we did in class. Do they seem to balance?

Draw or write what you put in the two bags.

Here's what I put in the first bag:

Here's what I put in the second bag:

To the Family

Finding Things That Balance

Math Content
Developing a sense of what's lighter and heavier by feel

Materials
Student Sheet 4
Pencil
Two grocery bags
Nonbreakable household goods

In class, students have been working to put together two groups of objects that weigh about the same. They judge the weight by feel, lifting the objects in two bags, one in each hand. For homework, your child will use objects found in your home—perhaps things from the kitchen—to make two bags that balance (weigh about the same). If the first attempt doesn't balance, your child can make adjustments by adding or removing objects. When the bags are balanced, your child will use pictures or words to record on the student sheet the objects that are in each bag.

Which Holds More?

We used container _____ and container _____ .

Which container holds more? _____

Draw a picture of the container that holds more.

How did you figure it out? _____

_____

We used container _____ and container _____ .

Which container holds more? _____

Draw a picture of the container that holds more.

How did you figure it out? _____

_____

Block Puzzle A

Which set of shapes fills the puzzle exactly? Try them both.

Which set of shapes exactly fills Puzzle A?_____

Set 1

Shape	⬡	⬟	▱	▢	▱	△
How many?	0	0	0	9	0	0

Set 2

Shape	⬡	⬟	▱	▢	▱	△
How many?	0	0	3	3	6	2

Optional Show how the blocks fit. Glue on paper shapes or color them in.

Block Puzzle B

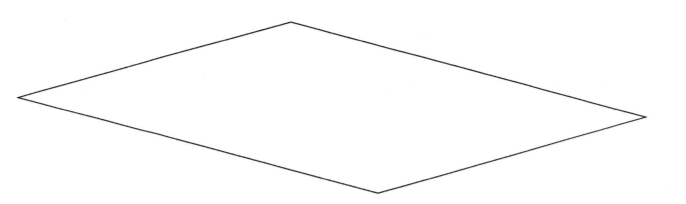

Which set of shapes fills the puzzle exactly? Try them both.

Which set of shapes exactly fills Puzzle B? _____

Set 1

Shape	⬡	⬡	▱	▢	▱	△
How many?	0	0	4	0	4	1

Set 2

Shape	⬡	⬡	▱	▢	▱	△
How many?	0	0	0	0	12	0

Optional Show how the blocks fit. Glue on paper shapes or color them in.

Block Puzzle C

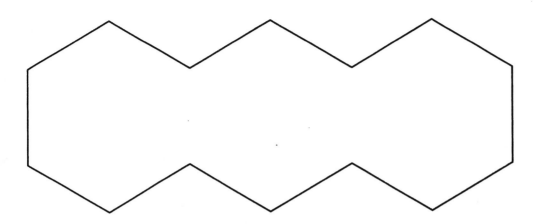

Which set of shapes fills the puzzle exactly? Try them both.

Which set of shapes exactly fills Puzzle C?_____

Set 1

Shape	⬡	⏢	▱	▢	▱	△
How many?	0	2	3	0	0	3

Set 2

Shape	⬡	⏢	▱	▢	▱	△
How many?	0	2	3	0	0	6

Optional Show how the blocks fit. Glue on paper shapes or color them in.

Block Puzzle D

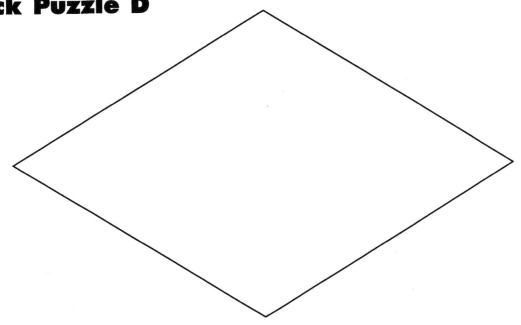

Which set of shapes fills the puzzle exactly? Try them both.

Which set of shapes exactly fills Puzzle D? _____

Set 1

Shape	⬡	⬠	▱	▢	▱	△
How many?	2	2	6	0	0	2

Set 2

Shape	⬡	⬠	▱	▢	▱	△
How many?	0	4	10	0	0	2

Optional Show how the blocks fit. Glue on paper shapes or color them in.

Block Puzzle E

Make your own puzzle.
Fill the outline.

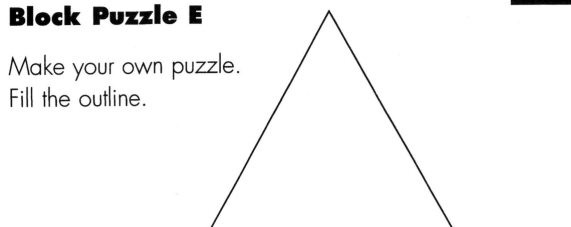

Write down how many blocks of each kind you used. Fill in the other chart with a set of blocks that does **not** solve the puzzle.

Set 1

Shape	⬡	⬡(trapezoid)	▱	□	▱	△
How many?						

Set 2

Shape	⬡	⬡(trapezoid)	▱	□	▱	△
How many?						

Block Puzzle F

Make your own puzzle.
Fill the outline.

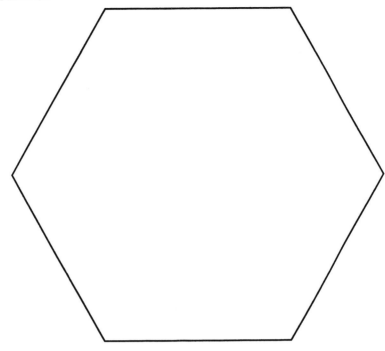

Write down how many blocks of each kind you used. Fill in the other chart with a set of blocks that does **not** solve the puzzle.

Set 1

Shape	⬡	⏢	▱	☐	▱	△
How many?						

Set 2

Shape	⬡	⏢	▱	☐	▱	△
How many?						

Which Holds More?

We used container _____ and container_____ .

Which container holds more?_____

Draw a picture of the container that holds more.

How did you figure it out?_____

_____

We used container _____ and container _____ .

Which container holds more?_____

Draw a picture of the container that holds more.

How did you figure it out?_____

_____

Name   Date
Student Sheet 12

Comparing Bottles

Use this sheet when you compare 5 bottles
to see how much water they hold.

Keeping track:

Which two bottles hold the same amount of water?

bottle _____ and bottle _____

Draw these two bottles here.

© Dale Seymour Publications®   **25**   *Investigation 2 • Sessions 5–7*
Bigger, Taller, Heavier, Smaller

Two Containers

Choose two empty containers. Find out
which holds more water.

You can use something to help you
fill them, such as a measuring cup, a spoon,
or a small paper cup.

Draw a picture of the two containers you used:

Write what you did and what you found out.

_____

_____

_____

_____

To the Family

Two Containers

Math Content
Comparing capacities of containers of different sizes

Materials
Student Sheet 13
Pencil
Two empty containers
Water (or something dry, such as sand or rice) to fill the containers
Small scoop (such as a paper cup, measuring cup, or spoon)

In class, students have been filling up containers with water, with sand, and with small plastic cubes, to compare how much containers of different shapes and sizes can hold. For homework, you child will find two containers at home and figure out which holds more by filling them with water, sand, rice, beans, or anything similar that is easy to pour. Your child may use a paper cup or some other small scoop to fill the larger containers. Find a place for your child to work, where spills don't matter. You might want to spread a newspaper on the work surface. Your child will record on the student sheet what the containers look like, what he or she did to compare them, and the results.

Foot Outlines from Home

As we study length, we are going to compare the lengths of different feet.

You need to trace outlines of at least four different feet. Bring your foot outlines back to school.

- Use a new sheet of paper for each foot. (Use any paper, even newspaper.)

- Use a pencil, crayon, or marker.

- Trace each foot with socks on, no shoes.

- Trace only one foot for each person. It doesn't matter which foot.

- Label each foot with the person's name.

- Cut out each outline.

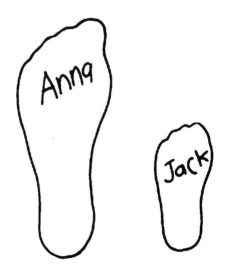

To the Family

Foot Outlines from Home

Math Content
Gathering materials for exploring length in class

Materials
Student Sheet 15
Large scrap paper
Pencil, crayon, or marker
Scissors

Students are starting to learn about length by comparing objects to see which is longer. In an upcoming class, we will compare the length of people's feet by looking at paper outlines of different feet. For homework, your chill will make some foot outlines to use for this activity. Follow the instructions on the student sheet, tracing one foot (in socks) of at least four people. If you can do even more, that will help provide outlines for children who are not able to find enough feet.

Shorter Than My Arm

Bring in two things from home to measure. They should be nonbreakable. Each thing should be shorter than your arm.

We will measure these things in math class.

What did you decide to bring?

_____

_____

To the Family

Shorter Than My Arm

Math Content
Gathering materials for exploring length

Materials
Student Sheet 17
Pencil

As we continue working with length, students will be using interlocking cubes to measure objects. We may find, for example, that a book is 11 cubes long. For homework, your child will look for two objects—each one shorter than your child's arm—to bring to class for these measuring activities. All objects will be returned, so please label them with your child's name.

Foot Match-Ups

Foot length   **Whose foot is a match?**

about 6 cubes long   _____

about 9 cubes long   _____

about 12 cubes long   _____

about 14 cubes long   _____

less than 6 cubes long   _____

more than 14 cubes long _____

Name _____   Date _____

Measuring with Hands and Feet

Find things to measure. What did you find?
Draw each object or write its name. How long is it?
Write its length. Circle the word (**hands** or **feet**)
that tells what you used for measuring.

Thing measured	Length	Measured with	
_____	_____	hands	feet
_____	_____	hands	feet
_____	_____	hands	feet
_____	_____	hands	feet
_____	_____	hands	feet
_____	_____	hands	feet
_____	_____	hands	feet
_____	_____	hands	feet

To the Family

Measuring with Hands and Feet

Math Content

Measuring and comparing lengths using nonstandard units

Materials

Student Sheet 16
Pencil

In class, students have been measuring length in various ways. They have measured objects in the classroom with cubes; they have compared objects (which things are longer or shorter than my pencil?); and they have been measuring out longer lengths using hands (wrist to fingertip) and feet (heel-to-toe baby steps). For homework, your child will measure several more objects at home with either hands or feet, just the way we did in class. On the student sheet, your child will record with either drawing or words what he or she measured, along with the length of each object written as a specific number of hands or feet.

How Many Cubes Long?

Name of object	Picture	How long
_____	_____	_____ cubes
_____	_____	_____ cubes
_____	_____	_____ cubes
_____	_____	_____ cubes
_____	_____	_____ cubes

Which is your longest object? _____

Which is your shortest object? _____

1	2	3	4	5	6	7	8	9	10
11	12	13	14	15	16	17	18	19	20
21	22	23	24	25	26	27	28	29	30
31	32	33	34	35	36	37	38	39	40
41	42	43	44	45	46	47	48	49	50
51	52	53	54	55	56	57	58	59	60
61	62	63	64	65	66	67	68	69	70
71	72	73	74	75	76	77	78	79	80
81	82	83	84	85	86	87	88	89	90
91	92	93	94	95	96	97	98	99	100

Investigation 1 Resource
Bigger, Taller, Heavier, Smaller

Ten Turns

Materials: One number cube
Counters (50–60)
Ten Turns Game Sheet

Players: 2

Object: With a partner, collect as many counters as you can.

How to Play

1. Roll the number cube. What number did you roll? Take that many counters to start your collection. Write the number you rolled and the total number you have. (For the first turn, these numbers are the same.)

2. On each turn, roll the number cube and take that many counters. Find the total number of counters you and your partner have together.

3. After each turn, write the number you rolled and the new total.

4. Play for 10 turns.

Variations

a. Play for fewer turns or more turns.

b. Roll two number cubes on each turn.

c. Instead of a number cube, use the Number Cards for 1 to 6. Mix them and turn up one at a time.

> **Note to Families**
>
> For counters, use buttons, pennies, paper clips, beans, or toothpicks. If you don't have a number cube or number cards, use slips of paper numbered 1–6. If you don't have the Ten Turns Game Sheet, keep track of the numbers for each turn and the new total on a blank sheet of paper.

Ten Turns Game Sheet

Turn 1.   I rolled _____.   Now we have _____.

Turn 2.   I rolled _____.   Now we have _____.

Turn 3.   I rolled _____.   Now we have _____.

Turn 4.   I rolled _____.   Now we have _____.

Turn 5.   I rolled _____.   Now we have _____.

Turn 6.   I rolled _____.   Now we have _____.

Turn 7.   I rolled _____.   Now we have _____.

Turn 8.   I rolled _____.   Now we have _____.

Turn 9.   I rolled _____.   Now we have _____.

Turn 10. I rolled _____.   Now we have _____.

Practice Page A

The number of the day is _____

Write equations that show ways
to make the number of the day.

Practice Page A

The number of the day is _____

Write equations that show ways
to make the number of the day.

Practice Page B

Nina has 17 yellow marbles.
She also has 5 green marbles.
How many marbles does she have?

Show how you solved this problem.
Use pictures, numbers, or words.

Name _____ Date _____

Practice Page C

Rico had 21 crackers. He ate 8 of them.
How many crackers did he have left?

Show how you solved this problem.
Use pictures, numbers, or words.

Practice Page D

Eric picked 19 flowers. He gave
12 flowers to his mother.
How many flowers did he have left?

Show how you solved this problem.
Use pictures, numbers, or words.

Practice Page E

Lexi collects stickers. She has 9 stars,
10 dinosaurs, and 6 hearts.
How many stickers does she have?

Show how you solved this problem.
Use pictures, numbers, or words.